Assessing Learners

Assessing Learners

Using the AASL Standards
to Measure Competency and Growth

ELIZABETH A. BURNS

ALA Editions

CHICAGO | 2023

American Association
of School Librarians

TRANSFORMING LEARNING

ELIZABETH A. BURNS, PhD, is an associate professor and the school library program director for the Library and Information Studies Program in the Darden College of Education and Professional Studies at Old Dominion University. She is a career educator who spent several years as a classroom teacher and school librarian before moving into higher education. She teaches library education courses, preparing graduate students for endorsement in school library media and careers in library and information workplaces. Her research focuses on curriculum and instruction, assessment, school library pedagogy, diversity and inclusion, and information literacy.

© 2023 by the American Library Association

Extensive effort has gone into ensuring the reliability of the information in this book; however, the publisher makes no warranty, express or implied, with respect to the material contained herein.

ISBN: 978-0-8389-4914-6 (paper)

Library of Congress Cataloging-in-Publication Data

Names: Burns, Elizabeth A., 1973- author.
Title: Assessing learners : using the AASL standards to measure competency and growth / Elizabeth A. Burns.
Description: Chicago : ALA Editions, 2023. | Includes bibliographical references and index. | Summary: "This professional guide provides current theories and assessment strategies for learning; ready-to-use styles of assessment relevant to those working in school libraries, with lessons that can be incorporated into their practice; and a bridge between student assessment and school librarian practice, aiding readers in their ongoing professional development"—Provided by publisher.
Identifiers: LCCN 2023016483 | ISBN 9780838949146 (paperback)
Subjects: LCSH: School libraries—Standards—United States. | School libraries—Aims and objectives—United States. | School librarian participation in curriculum planning—United States. | School libraries—Activity programs—United States—Evaluation. | Library orientation for school children—United States—Evaluation. | Libraries and schools—United States. | Libraries and students—United States. | Education—Standards—United States.
Classification: LCC Z675.S3 B85 2023 | DDC 027.80973—dc23/eng/20230601
LC record available at https://lccn.loc.gov/2023016483

Book design by Alejandra Diaz in the Utopia Std and Galano typefaces

♾ This paper meets the requirements of ANSI/NISO Z39.48-1992 (Permanence of Paper).

Printed in the United States of America
27 26 25 24 23   5 4 3 2 1

This book is dedicated to
my three children who constantly remind me
of all the ways success can be viewed and measured differently.
I am forever proud to have learned from each of you.

And to all the school librarians showing up for their students every day—
you are forever my inspiration!

CONTENTS

Learner Assessment in the School Library

School librarians are teachers and instructional partners. In these roles, they are part of the educational team responsible for learner academic success. Assessment is a key component of teaching and learning in the school library. Assessment directs the instruction by educators and informs and improves learner understanding. The American Association of School Librarians (AASL) affirms the instructional role of school librarians (AASL 2020) and through the *National School Library Standards for Learners, School Librarians, and School Libraries* emphasizes their responsibility to prepare all learners for college, career, and life as essential to the profession (AASL 2018b, 12). For school librarians to fully embrace their role as educators in the school environment, measuring student achievement and ensuring appropriate instructional strategies through learner assessment is essential. Equally true of the school library as it is in all learning environments of the school, assessments must be developed that measure learning progress. In the school library, this measurement includes evidence of library and information skills:

- Critical thinking, problem solving, and metacognition
- Creativity and exploration of personal and academic pursuits
- Communication and collaboration
- Proficiency with information literacies
- Life skills and personal responsibility necessary for living in the world

Learner progress and growth in these areas naturally align with the mission of the school library and prepare all learners for future success.

Assessment Guided by the AASL Standards

The *National School Library Standards* use a competency-based approach to measure professional instruction and personalized learner growth within the school library. The AASL Standards are framed by four Domains—Think, Create, Share, and Grow—and their Competencies within six Shared Foundations—Inquire, Include, Collaborate, Curate, Explore, and Engage. This structure is presented in three integrated frameworks for learners, school librarians, and school libraries. The Competencies demonstrated in the *AASL Standards Framework for Learners* offer an approach different from that of previous, objective-based standards. Not designed as curriculum, the learner Competencies of the integrated frameworks heavily focus on the learning process and align with the ideals of personalized learning that ground best practice in the school library.

The school librarian fills a unique position in the school building. The school librarian works with each learner in the school and is a teaching peer to each educator. Unlike most other resource educators, the school librarian must be familiar with all the curricula of the school. The school librarian supports the school-wide curriculum through the resources provided in the school library collection (print and digital) and through engagement of integrated instruction support. In these ways, the school librarian infuses the Competencies presented in the *AASL Standards Framework for Learners* into collaboratively planned, content-driven lessons.

Assessment Aligned with the Learning Domains

The four learning Domains that help organize the Competencies in the AASL Standards frameworks—Think, Create, Share, and Grow—acknowledge and address the different learning activities that may take place in the school library learning environment. Though often aligned with several learner Competencies, an integrated school library experience frequently meets the intent of one learning Domain over the others.

Lessons that align with the cognitive learning Domain *Think* employ the Competencies that require learners to think critically and gain knowledge. Lessons that align with the psychomotor learning Domain *Create* require a more constructivist approach to information. Here learners are tasked to draw conclusions, make informed decisions, apply knowledge in new ways, and create new meaning. Lessons that primarily align with the affective learning Domain *Share* allow learners to embrace opportunities to share and participate with others. Finally, lessons that align with the developmental learning Domain *Grow* demonstrate a commitment to fostering a growth mindset and support pursuits of personal growth (AASL 2018a, 15).

It is important that learners have an opportunity to participate within each of the learning Domains. These interactions help prepare learners for active engagement with information as well as with others in a learning community. Interactions through the various learning Domains help prepare K–12 learners for college, career, and community (AASL 2018a, 15–16).

Lessons Developed Across Shared Foundations

The Shared Foundations in the AASL Standards—Inquire, Include, Collaborate, Curate, Explore, and Engage—inform the library learning objectives of a lesson. The student-friendly language of the standards can help inform simple statements that explicitly dictate what a learner will know or be able to do at the end of a lesson or learning experience. Rarely does a lesson focus on the skills, knowledge, and understanding found in the Competencies of just one Shared Foundation. More frequently, a well-developed lesson will include Competencies from two or more Shared Foundations. Though each Shared Foundation *can* stand alone as an area of focus, when integrated, the six Shared Foundations help form growth experiences that engage learners in thoughtful, productive, and inclusive lessons (AASL 2018a, 44).

Further emphasis is given when also determining the learning Domain met by a lesson. The learning Domains allow learners to showcase their learning within the Shared Foundations and along different steps in the growth process.

Using This Book to Explore Learner Assessment

Assessment is a critical component of effective instruction. This book focuses on the use of assessment in the school library. Each of chapters 2–6 is dedicated to a type of assessment— diagnostic, formative, summative, self, and virtual. Within each chapter, a brief overview of the assessment type further defines and situates assessment practices in the school library setting. Each chapter then introduces and explores assessment models used in school library instruction. The assessments in this book can be used as stand-alone assessments, designed to measure learner growth and understanding at one point in time. They also may be used as part of a larger unit or series of instructional tasks.

"Assessment in Action" Scenarios

Scenario-based examples of assessment in action accompany many of the assessment tools and strategies described throughout the chapters. The In Action scenarios situate the assessments at various grade levels and in the context of integrated learner experiences that would occur in a school library setting. Learning scenarios and assessments are framed with the learner Competencies of the Shared Foundations, helping demonstrate the scope and sequence of the use of assessment tools in the school library.

Each scenario presents a part of a lesson or series of lessons aligned with at least one learner Competency, which guides the design of the assessment featured. Several scenarios include Competencies within multiple Shared Foundations to demonstrate the connected nature of these learning targets, but within one learning Domain to demonstrate focused learning tasks. Each assessment scenario describes construction of a school library lesson to include authentic tasks that build toward mastery. Learning tasks are evaluated with assessments aligned with the identified learner Competencies and school library objectives. Assessment tools or strategies introduced within the chapter are exemplified through these scenarios and described within the learning context of an integrated library lesson objective.

Integrated Instruction

Effective instruction in school libraries is rarely presented as a set of isolated skills. The most meaningful instruction in a school library integrates other content-area curricula and allows for collaboration with other teaching peers throughout the school. The Assessment in Action scenarios presented in this book reflect the Competencies from the *AASL Standards Framework for Learners* together with the following national content-area standards:

- College, Career, and Civic Life (C3) Framework for Social Studies State Standards (2013)
- Common Core State Standards (CCSS) for English Language Arts (2010)
- ISTE Standards for Students (2016)
- Next Generation (NextGen) Science Standards (2013)

The inclusion of content-area standards throughout the book showcases authentic use of the assessments and connects learning taking place in the school library to learning elsewhere in the school building. Each scenario highlights integrated instruction, supporting content-area collaboration and revealing ways in which different strategies may be used or modified to meet a school librarian's need to assess learner progress within an integrated instructional unit developed with a collaborative teaching peer.

Assessment for Innovating Instruction

Although this book is independent from the material presented in the AASL Standards text, several components complement, support, or further describe the Competencies of the *AASL Standards Framework for Learners*. Like the AASL Standards themselves, the assessments in this book do not emphasize discrete skills that must be mastered before progress can be made to the next set of content; assessment is rarely finite. Instead, types of assessments are presented as engaging opportunities, and these opportunities are showcased within specific integrated curricular scenarios. Each can be modified with additional rigor and resources to measure different kinds of learning and a variety of challenges across years and learning experiences. Competency-based education and the way assessment is informed through personalized instruction initiatives frame the discussion. Ideally, the ideas presented will be a beginning, inspiring new and innovative assessment ideas for your own learners and school library setting.

Assessing Learner Process and Progress

Assessment in the school library is less product, or skill, oriented than in other areas of the educational curriculum and more focused on process. It is aligned with the informational, discovery, motivational, or innovative learning that is often the guiding tenet of learning in the school library. This approach requires a unique look at assessment tools and practices that are especially beneficial to the library learning environment. School librarians must shift the context of what assessment looks like and how it is implemented within the school library, allowing learners to develop critical-thinking and problem-solving skills and creativity, leading to mastery of their learning process.

The *AASL Standards Framework for Learners* and the learning Domains—Think, Create, Share, and Grow—mirror the different types of learning students do as they progress through information activities from kindergarten through high school. It is essential to plan for the assessment of this progression and for personalized learner development and growth in ways that feel authentic to their learning and their lives. This chapter considers the complex nature of assessing competency across developmental levels while scaffolding authentic tasks to encourage growth mindset.

A Shift from Traditional Assessment

Traditionally, assessment practices included lots of worksheets and educator-driven tests and assignments. Many occurred at the end of lessons that focused on skills taught in isolation, without much connection or relationship to authentic, real-world information tasks. These assessments measure discrete, objective facts rather than the process and progress learners make in understanding authentic information-seeking behaviors. Traditional assessments fell out of favor as teaching practices turned away from isolated library skills and toward integrated library instruction. Most traditional assessments run counter to the personal growth and the progress of competency-based instruction that the *National School Library Standards* support. Some additional critiques contend that traditional assessments

- create a competitive learning culture,
- deemphasize progress,
- are rarely an accurate representation of learner ability, and
- do not foster risk taking.

Further, the language associated with "grading," a common feature of traditional assessments, often has a negative connotation. Grading shuts down the learning process and does not celebrate individual learner success and progress. In many traditional assessments, the educator communicates to learners that they are *right* or *wrong*, rather than progressing in their understanding.

Additionally, because grades (in the numerical or traditional format of A, B, C) are often conflated with nonlearning elements, they rarely demonstrate or capture meaningful learner progress. A learner's ability to read an assessment, read and respond to vocabulary that may or may not be associated with assessed content, or maintain attention to an assessment task are all examples of elements of learning that may be present on a traditional assessment and that do not measure the library learning objective. Further, rigor is frequently misunderstood by educators and presented as additional work, with some educators believing that lengthier assessments or assignments demonstrate additional skill or understanding. But rigor does not correlate to the amount of work. Assessments should be designed that appropriately scaffold demonstrated learning and measure the difficulty of the task or the intellectual challenge. Because of the assessment culture that emerged in schools, some educators lost sight of what was most important—measuring learning. Although traditional assessment practices are misguided, it may take a bit of deprogramming to see assessment through a different lens.

Assessment Without Grades

Measuring growth and progress is an important component of school library instruction. Unlike many educators, the school librarian typically does not assign a numeric grade and is not responsible for end-of-year standardized testing. Instead, the focus of assessment in the school library may take nontraditional forms such as identifying individual learner strengths and weaknesses in progression toward a skill or determined knowledge base; providing career-focused interests; developing information-seeking and research skills, problem-solving skills, and written or oral communication skills; and assessing transferable skills that learners may continue to develop for future endeavors.

Traditional grades rarely account for individual growth. For example, a gifted learner who does little work may receive the same letter grade as a struggling learner who has improved steadily throughout the course or a learner who started off strongly but performed poorly in the last quarter. In each of these scenarios, all three learners may end up with the same letter *grade*, but the effort taken to arrive there and the conversations that should have taken place between educator and learner would likely be very different. In the school library, without the requirement to assign grades, a focus on growth can be encouraged and enables the school librarian to give each learner feedback tailored to their specific progress, helping each learner grow toward future success.

Competency-Based Assessment

The *National School Library Standards* are conceptual standards. The developed Competencies of the AASL Standards are not curriculum and should not be defined or read as such. When planning lessons and assessments aligned with the standards, it is important to note that the AASL Standards were designed from a competency-based approach. Student learning outcomes developed from the standards should be skills or knowledge that can be assessed and measured.

From Outcomes to Competency-Based Performance Assessments

Previous sets of standards, across the educational landscape, have relied on an outcomes-based model. Outcomes-based education models focus on learners' mastery of knowledge or demonstration of use. Outcomes-based education derives from educational models that support allowing the time and instruction necessary for the majority of a given set of learners to master a skill. This approach is the product of traditional teaching models and K–12 school libraries that adhere to fixed schedules and rely on skills lessons taught in isolation, with limited or no collaboration with teaching peers. This antiquated model of school library instruction focuses on "just in case" instruction, teaching rote skills that learners *may* need if presented with an arbitrary task, rather than "just in time" authentic tasks taught when learners have a genuine need or desire for learning. Outcomes-based learning is further complicated in that assessing mastery can be challenging. It can be difficult to determine whether a learner has, in fact, mastered a skill. These challenges have gradually led to more competence-based approaches in instruction and assessment, including

- developing clear outcomes for each learning task,
- identifying how learners can demonstrate progress through actions and performance,

- developing flexible and personalized time frames based on learner needs, and
- allowing for fluid time frames that approach learning tasks when needed.

Performance-based assessments have gained popularity as demonstrations of knowledge in all K–12 environments. They are particularly aligned with the values of the school library. A strength of competency-based education is that it is highly focused on the learning progress and growth of the individual learner. When considering assessments for the school library, authentic, performance-based assessments focus more on what learners can *do* rather than how learners demonstrate knowledge.

Frequently performance assessments require learners to perform a task or create a product. This output is then evaluated in a formative manner during the progression of the task or at the end as a summative assessment using a developed set of criteria. These authentic performance assessments frequently mirror what might occur in a real-life situation that the learner would encounter, making the task particularly relevant. To be most effective, the assessment would have multiple right answers or be open ended to allow for maximum student choice and engagement.

Assessment in the school library conducted with a competency-based performance approach produces an increased student commitment to learning. This type of assessment doesn't look at all student work the same because every learner has the potential to begin and end in a different place. Assessments are an integral part of instruction and assist the school librarian in documenting learner progress. The instructional purpose and goal, frequently defined by a student learning objective for a lesson, help identify the most appropriate assessment tool.

A Competency-Based Approach to Mastery Learning

Learner assessment in the school library can also show that taking a risk and not succeeding does not mean learners are failing: it means they need to try another way. Many educators approach learning in terms of skills taught in discrete spans of time. Instead, competency-based learning and assessment can be thought of as an approach to mastery. We want learners to apply their understanding of skills in a progression from novice to proficient (often supported), then gradually remove these supports to achieve full independence and mastery.

The move to mastery learning is often compared to a skill like riding a bike. You begin with instruction and modeling—or an explanation of how the bike pedals and brakes work, a demonstration of the functions, and so on. The rider then progresses to having someone hold the bike while starting the ride or having training wheels on the bike, which is comparable to a novice level. The rider is learning and can complete the task but needs help and guidance. Once the rider can ride without training wheels or help, they have reached proficiency. They are able to ride for a short distance but may need to recalibrate, stop, and adjust frequently on shorter trips. After they have been riding awhile and can ride for long distances or, most importantly, can ride different bikes, they have achieved mastery. The key is that the skill is transferable. You can take this pattern of progression and apply it to any type of learning.

Assessment Supporting Personalized Learning

"The goal of competency-based education is to support learners' growth through personalized learning experiences" (AASL 2018b, 19). Competency-based education starts with the identification of a set of competencies—such as those identified in the *AASL Standards Framework for Learners*—and enables learners to develop mastery of each competency at their own personalized pace. In the case of the *National School Library Standards*, this mastery process happens over time with the assistance of the school librarian. It represents a break from previous models in which learning was presented in specific sets or grade bands, suggesting that all learners must master one skill or concept at a given age or grade level before they might be presented with the next set of content or progress to the next level of complexity on a skill. Personalized learning is foundational to the Inquiry process and to the support of reading, two of the key attributes of a well-developed and effective K–12 library program. Personalized learning allows learners to demonstrate progress and understanding of concepts and skills at an individual pace.

However, there are some misconceptions about personalized learning. Personalized learning does not mean that learners work by themselves or independently. It also does not mean that each learner is working on a different skill or task at one time. Personalized learning does focus on individual students and allows learners to become more engaged. It includes collaborative competencies whereby learners identify what interests them and how they best learn, as well as different people they can learn from, which may include peers and others in the community in addition to educators. Learners must have the skills and knowledge to be successful in any type of assessment that is used in a school library setting. This assessment may include consideration of background content knowledge prior to the lesson occurring with the school librarian.

The AASL Standards support this personal learning approach. Each of the learner Competencies presented in the *AASL Standards Framework for Learners* can be addressed at any point in a learner's academic education, with no set or correct point of entry. School librarians establish learning expectations based on the Competencies, and learners are afforded the opportunity to express voice and choice in some components of what they learn. This approach leads to greater engagement with information as learners explore topics of relevance and interest.

The school library can be the ideal place for personalized learning. Not only are there abundant and various resources but there is also adaptable space and opportunity to develop the inquiry process. The same resource is not ideal for all learners. Some may need materials at different reading levels or in various formats, such as those with audio support or larger fonts, more-complex vocabulary, or material dedicated to different topics of interest. A quality collection that has been well curated can provide this type of personalized learning. Additionally, the availability of online resources ensures that learners have access to resources at their point of need and in the format that is most beneficial. The addition of makerspaces and alternative forms of resources further ensures that learners have access to the materials that will provide personalized opportunity for success. These resources also increase the opportunity for collaboration and iterative processes.

Fostering a Growth Mindset through Authentic Assessment

Carol Dweck's book *Mindset* (2006) introduced and brought an educational focus to the personalized learning that is infused into the *National School Library Standards*. Through this lens, assessment becomes a conversation between the school librarian and learner that facilitates an understanding of what the learner already knows, what the learner can do, and what needs further work. Even more importantly, this type of assessment directs the learner to understand how to make improvements and how to recognize when legitimate growth has occurred.

When considering assessment in the school library, it is critical to consider the shift from demonstrating arbitrary facts and isolated skills to monitoring authentic tasks encountered through the use of information. These authentic assessments (figure 1.1) assist learners to become effective and independent users of ideas and information.

Authentic assessment allows the school librarian to measure learner achievement of learning objectives and alter instruction as needed to better meet learning targets. To encourage creative thinking and personal growth, assessment in the school library focuses on opportunities to engage in a process of learning that allows learners to create their own responses, products, and synthesis of knowledge rather than select from answers that have already been determined. This approach increases the likelihood that information tasks replicate the types of challenges and opportunities that learners will face in the real world.

Feedback directing learner effort makes learning better. The goal for learners is to increase their independent skills from introduction to proficiency to final stages of mastery learning of knowledge, skills, and information tasks. Assessment offers opportunities to revise and progress toward mastery learning. For this

FIGURE 1.1

Revised Bloom's Taxonomy for authentic assessment

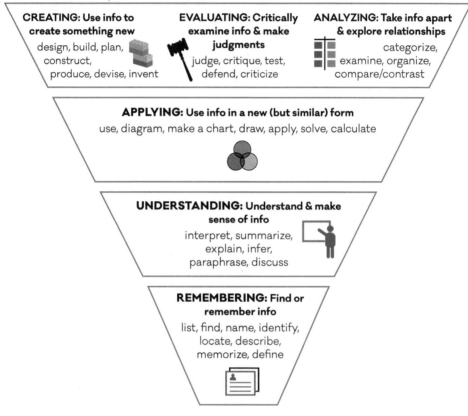

Source: Bloom's Example © Rawia Inaim is licensed under a CC BY-SA (Attribution ShareAlike) license: creativecommons.org/licenses/by-sa/4.0/.

reason, assessment in the school library often values engagement. When using a more competency-based approach, learners become more intrinsically motivated because the numeric grade, or external motivation, is removed. This approach aligns with authentic learning practices because learning activities typically don't prepare learners for tests; they prepare learners for life skills and interactions. When engagement and assessment in the school library are developed to measure authentic information needs, learners prepare to attack and solve problems using their knowledge and skills (figure 1.2).

Every learning experience should support progress toward the learner's achievement. The school librarian should consider deliberate ways to make all learning substantial and to connect content and library skills to what is relevant in the learner's life. Through these varied experiences and feedback, learners can practice essential skills that will propel them to mastery.

FIGURE 1.2

Authentic learning and assessments

Assessments are aligned with an information need, discovery, personal motivation, or innovative learning.

In the school library, assessments should target:

| Critical thinking, problem solving, and metacognition | Creativity and exploration of personal and academic pursuits | Communication and collaboration | Proficiency with information literacies | Life skills and personal responsibility necessary for living in the world |

Information skills are most meaningful when learned while addressing an authentic, real-world need for information. Effective school library lessons bring together opportunity for personal learner progress, feedback from the school librarian, and alignment with the AASL learner Competencies and include

- an identified school library objective or learning task that supports the AASL learner Competencies,
- detailed, authentic learning activities that engage all learners and provide for a positive learning environment,
- assessments aligned with the developed school library learning objectives, and
- suggestions to differentiate instruction and accommodate *all* learners.

Although the school librarian may co-assess with the content-area educator, school librarians typically focus more on *process* whereas the content educator may focus more on the final *product*.

Obstacles to Growth Assessment

One way to overcome outdated assessment practices is to revise teaching and learning practices. School library lessons that are most effective include real-world application of information-seeking practices and critical thinking and information use. School librarians no longer spend full periods lecturing: this is not an efficient use of class time if learners are to master content effectively. Employing effective collaboration and technology integration is a better use of time and allows the school librarian to become more of a coach and a facilitator. Learners can more effectively practice skills and develop competencies by participating in hands-on learning tasks than by viewing slide deck presentations crammed with content.

A goal of assessment is to make these skills transferable, so the time you invest will pay huge dividends throughout the year as well as in encouraging lifelong learning. Time is always going to be a challenge, but many skills can be taught through the learning and assessment process. Providing effective feedback about learning and encouraging self-evaluation are two of the most important elements of assessment in a school library focused on process. Assessment embedded into instruction allows for active engagement and immediate redirection of understanding and aids in instructional practices.

Some educators believe authentic assessments are too subjective. Creative or process-driven assessments allow more learner voice in determining progress and work quality. However, there is seldom only one right way to do anything. Learners need opportunities to synthesize learning. This need should be encouraged in a way that is intuitive. All learning is subjective, and when only one chance or route for learning is offered, the possibility that every learner will achieve mastery is greatly limited.

Isolated Instruction

Instruction in the school library is most beneficial when planned collaboratively with teaching peers and integrated with other content curriculum. Skills taught without connection to a learning need are rarely transferable. Learning is most beneficial when situated in context. Assessment of personal growth can then be measured. Though co-teaching may be the "gold standard" for this collaboration, given scheduling and other environmental barriers, it is frequently not possible that both the school librarian and teaching peer can teach the same group of learners in the same space at the same time. Collaboration with others can still occur, and library content should be integrated with other skills and objectives to provide a meaningful learning experience. In collaborative, *integrated* instruction, it is still essential that more than content be assessed. The library components of each integrated lesson should be assessed for understanding and growth.

School library assessment in an integrated lesson may frequently be overlooked or misunderstood. Assessment requires a negotiation with collaborative partners. Frequently, only a final product or task is considered assessment. It is critical that all stages of the process are considered, evaluated, and subjected to feedback along the way. During collaborative meetings, participants should discuss who will be assessing specific skills and concepts and who will provide learner feedback. The types and models of formative assessment that will be used should also be negotiated at this time. Both content standards and library learning competencies should be included when measuring progress toward meeting the goals of each. This consideration will ensure that learners have opportunities to calibrate their learning prior to submission of any final learning tasks.

Determination of Mastery

Assessing mastery of library skills is challenging. In designing assessments that align with your school library objectives, consider these questions:

- What should learners know or be able to do?
- What might indicate that learners have met the stated goal?
- What does appropriate progress on this task look like?

Key components of effective competency-based education are competencies that may be developed into measurable and transferable learning objectives that empower learners. These learning objectives should include active language and incorporate learner voice and choice in the learning and assessment processes. Learners should receive timely, differentiated feedback and support based on their learning progress and needs. Finally, learning outcomes should include knowledge application or creation, or both; learners should be provided the opportunity to demonstrate critical-thinking skills and ways to demonstrate the use of a skill in future applications.

Language That Is Not Learner-Friendly

Standards are written using lots of terms learners don't always readily understand. To help learners assess their progress and personal growth, it is important to put learner competencies into student-friendly language. One way to help learners know their strengths and discover what they don't know is to ask them to apply skills and knowledge to new situations without help. When they have reached mastery level, they can take learning from one situation and apply it appropriately to another without prompting.

This language learning process should be transparent. Even with young learners, school librarians can explain what the standards are and what role they will play in the learning experience. Learners can take part in drafting student-friendly language. When learners are more aware of the purpose for learning, they are more likely to be engaged in learning. Create student-friendly language as a class activity on chart paper or sentence strips and then transfer the results to anchor charts or "touch" assessment graphics for regular use. You can also create an evolving anchor display of the standards you address and then have learners refer to this chart when they are working or reflecting on their progress.

FIGURE 1.3

AASL Standards language for learners

SHARED FOUNDATION I. INQUIRE

A. THINK: Learners display curiosity and initiative by:

Standards Language	Student Language
1. *Formulating* questions about a personal interest or a *curricular* topic.	1. I can write questions that help me find information I am looking for (for school or my own interest).
2. *Recalling* prior and *background knowledge* as *context* for new meaning.	2. I build on information I already know when I learn something new.

The school librarian can model the process by drafting new language for Shared Foundation I, Inquire. This exercise helps learners unpack the standards and capture the essence in their own words. Read the first standard aloud, break it apart if needed, and rewrite the standard in simple language. Think aloud while you rewrite and then have learners participate in the process (figure 1.3). Once learners have a version written in student-friendly language, they are ready to deploy the standard in the learning process.

Invest in Learner Assessment and Process

Good assessment practices equally blend the roles of teaching, learning, and evaluating. The best instruction happens when learners are part of the learning and assessment process. Measurement of authentic skills boosts learner engagement and allows the learner to be more invested in the instruction and in the learning process. This investment not only allows learners to monitor their progress but also allows both the learner and school librarian to determine understanding and growth.

Assessment in the school library is not new, but it is continually evolving. As school librarians overcome outdated perceptions of their position and establish their role as educators who support student academic achievement, a greater focus is given to implementing assessment practices to measure learner growth and value learning as a process.

As you explore the assessment types and strategies presented in this book, let the principles of competency-based learning, personalization, growth mindset, and authentic assessment be your guide. You *can* break the mold of traditional assessment in your learning community and inspire your educator peers to develop learners who become masters of their own learning.

Diagnostic Assessments

Diagnostic assessments are one type of formative assessment. Just as the name implies, the school librarian is attempting to diagnose the level of skill or understanding that learners have with new or upcoming material. Therefore, a diagnostic assessment is primarily given before any teaching or learning has occurred. Diagnostic assessments are preassessments used to aid school librarians and other educators as they evaluate the strengths and weaknesses of learners' knowledge, skills, and understanding about a specific set of information prior to instruction.

Diagnostic assessments play an important role in instruction in the school library. These assessments allow the school librarian to establish a baseline for where learner knowledge begins and to set goals and expectations for the learning that will occur. Additionally, diagnostic assessments help determine the depth and type of instruction that may be required on a given topic as well as any differentiation that may be necessary for all learners to be successful. In this way, the diagnostic assessment measures each learner's prior knowledge and informs the school librarian's teaching strategies. This information is particularly useful in a setting such as the school library, where learners may not visit regularly and skill development may take place across multiple visits or even years.

Diagnostic assessments also aid in formulating differentiation strategies. This approach helps ensure that all learners are provided the best opportunities, resources, and instruction for success. When used effectively, these assessments can inform decisions about resource selection, peer or instructor grouping and scaffolding, and method of delivery for whole-class or subgroup instruction.

Finally, use of diagnostic tools allows for maximum use of instructional time. If all learners can demonstrate some level of proficiency on a diagnostic assessment, there is no need for a school librarian to spend extensive time teaching these skills in a comprehensive library lesson. It may be sufficient to provide a brief review and then build on the concepts to further engage learners in more-complex and -rigorous tasks.

Often when using diagnostic assessments, the educator gives the identical assessment to learners after instruction as a post-test or postassessment to evaluate or compare gains in learner knowledge or measure the impact of instruction on learner progress toward meeting the stated lesson objective(s). In this chapter, we will explore diagnostic assessment tools that a school librarian commonly uses to develop instructional approaches for learner achievement. We will review the following diagnostic assessment tools:

- Pretest quiz
- Sort
- K-W-L chart
- Concept map

Pretest Quiz

The pretest quiz is a nongraded tool used to assess prior knowledge (figure 2.1). These assessments frequently are developed and administered in a traditional standardized assessment format. The pretest quiz is used to determine baseline knowledge and covers information and material the learner is not expected to know. The format of a pretest quiz can vary from a traditional pencil-and-paper arrangement to a digital version, most often using closed responses such as multiple choice, true or false (T/F), or fill-in-the-blank answers.

FIGURE 2.1
Example pretest quiz

1. Is this book fiction or nonfiction?

2. Is this book fiction or nonfiction?

3. What does an illustrator do?
   a. Writes the book
   b. Draws the pictures in a book
   c. Puts the book on the library shelf

ASSESSMENT IN ACTION
INFORMATION SORT

Fourth-grade readers are reviewing their knowledge of literary genres, as well as organization and location of materials in the school library, as they select new materials to read for academic and personal interest. This sort of diagnostic assessment prepares learners to meet integrated English/language arts and library lesson objectives.

AASL Standards Framework for Learners

V.A.1. Learners develop and satisfy personal curiosity by reading widely and deeply in multiple formats and write and create for a variety of purposes.

CCSS: English Language Arts—Literacy

RL.4.10. By the end of the year, read and comprehend literature, including stories, dramas, and poetry, in the grades 4–5 text complexity band proficiently, with scaffolding as needed at the high end of the range.

To determine how well learners are already able to identify genre, as well as location and organization of school library materials, a sort can be used with either physical library resources or images of resources. It can also be done online if technology allows. Learners organize the resources provided given specific criteria. On the basis of the results, the school librarian determines how much instruction is needed for each genre, as well as characteristics that help identify location of materials, such as call number, cataloging, and special markings. A sort is a useful diagnostic tool to determine how much learners know and how much instruction will be needed when introducing more-complex skills.

Sort

A common tool used to assess young learners, though it can be used at any age, is a sort. A sort asks the learner to organize material into two or more categories of information based on the learning content. This assessment task allows learners to quickly demonstrate their knowledge of the material and also allows for a quick visual scan by the school librarian to assess the accuracy of learner knowledge.

This assessment is particularly well suited for early learners because it can be adapted for nonreaders. A nonliterate sort can use manipulatives, or it can use paper but include pictures or objects in addition to, or instead of, words to aid and assess those learners who are not yet able to read or are not confident in reading.

K-W-L Chart

The K-W-L chart is designed to be used throughout the learning process. It aids learner organization of information before, during, and after instruction. The chart consists of three columns labeled K (know), W (wonder), and L (learn). The initial deployment, completion of the K or *know* column, can serve as the diagnostic assessment. Completion of the K column diagnoses, or determines, a learner's prior knowledge in addition to engaging and exciting the learner about the topic. This assessment can be completed individually or collaboratively in small groups or as a whole class. A frequent component of this assessment strategy is built-in time for shared responses, during which the school librarian may share or create a master list or chart to document common understanding. This exercise allows the school librarian to assess learner knowledge as well as redirect any incorrect or misleading information before progressing into the next stages of instruction.

The W column often begins an inquiry process, with learners developing questions of *wonder*. This exercise again may be done independently, in small groups, or as a larger class discussion. Finally, at the conclusion of instruction, and perhaps serving as a postassessment, the final column L, or *learn*, can be completed to document learner growth.

Concept Map

A concept map is a visual diagram that shows the connections and relationships of understanding between ideas (figure 2.2). The concept map functions as a pre-teaching strategy whereby learners can share what they already know about a given topic in a visual format. This strategy can be described as purposeful brainstorming. Learners are asked to interpret or demonstrate their understanding by connecting new ideas or topics to information they may already be familiar with. Learners can create or add to a map as an introduction is provided and their prior knowledge is activated.

The school librarian can model the creation of a map. Each new circle is referred to as a *node* and houses one concept in the map. The connecting lines are frequently called *arcs*. Sometimes an arc has an arrowhead to define direction.

Concept maps can be helpful in determining what is already known about a topic, as well as aiding to narrow focus on broader ideas and concepts. This assessment guides learners through the thinking process to establish and confirm prior knowledge before in-depth instruction begins.

FIGURE 2.2

Example concept map

Place a topic of investigation in the center circle. Fill connecting circles (as many as needed) with words or pictures that expand ideas about the main topic.

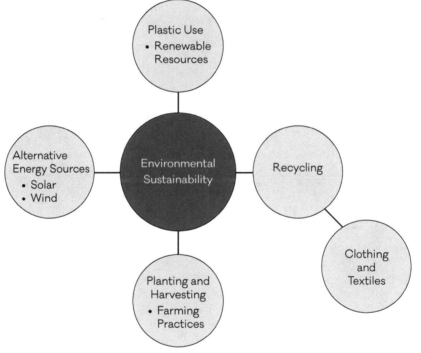

3

Formative Assessments

Formative assessments track learner progress and provide immediate feedback for learners and the school librarian. This feedback informs the instructional decisions and actions for continued growth. Formative assessments function as touch points to help educators determine whether learners understand key concepts and identify areas that need further attention.

Formative assessments provide a low-stakes opportunity to measure learner progress before a more-formalized evaluation. These checkups frequently are done quickly and informally. Formative assessments used for this purpose are generally checked or reviewed rather than traditionally graded, so that the school librarian and potential teaching peer can quickly determine learner progress—either individually or as an entire class. These snapshot results allow the school librarian to monitor the pace and depth of understanding toward the learning objectives.

This goal often means that formative assessment is conducted while learners are in the process of engaging with the material. The assessment is used to determine what comes next—for the learner, as well as for the school librarian. This type of assessment answers these questions:

- Does the learner understand the learning that has already occurred?
- Are we ready to move on to a new or more advanced concept?
- Is there a learner or group of learners that might benefit from more or different types of instruction at this point in the lesson?

The assessments provide timely feedback to learners and school librarians throughout the instructional process.

In the school library, because assessment does focus heavily on the process of learning, there is an expectation that learners will build on the skills they obtain and transfer that growth to the next learning task. Formative assessment practices allow school librarians to monitor learning along a continuum and gauge retention, as well as identify areas of learning that may be beneficial to review.

Good formative assessment can be tricky because it requires a balance between knowing that learners have reached a level of understanding and are ready to progress and identifying when the school librarian may need to develop a different approach for delivering the information. This process allows the school librarian to determine which learners are ready to move on and which may need additional or varied instruction. For this reason, it is not uncommon to include more than one formative assessment strategy within a given lesson. This strategy allows for several opportunities to check in with learners to measure progress.

There are a variety of formative assessment tasks that are effective at measuring learner growth and instructional progress. In this chapter, we will explore formative assessment tools that a school librarian commonly uses to develop instructional approaches for learner achievement. Because constructivist learning also frequently includes collaborative learning opportunities, this chapter also explores formative strategies to assess group learning opportunities. Finally, we'll explore reflection on the learning process as a means to assess progress. We will explore the following formative assessment tools commonly used in the school library:

- Quizzes and polls
- Conferences and interviews
- Observation and note charts
- Exit tickets
- Graphic organizers
- Group or collaborative assessment tools
- Reflective assessments

Quizzes and Polls

Polls and quizzes can provide a quick, and often fun, snapshot of how learners are progressing. These assessments can be conducted with a whole group but can also document individual learner scores to demonstrate personalized learning. This feature allows for assessment at both the individual and aggregate levels. Because the school librarian develops the questions, varying the difficulty of the questions provides opportunity for critical thinking and differentiation within the assessment. A variety of polls and quizzes can be used, and many popular formats require technology, though if you do not have a technology-rich environment you could modify these to be used without.

Each of these digital assessment tools does require advance preparation. The school librarian may need to create a class account or separate learner accounts to utilize some of the more-advanced features or the most interactive components and features. As is best practice with any tool or strategy, modeling effective use is also encouraged until learners become accustomed to the expectations. Create the assessment questions prior to the lesson, and then embed the quiz or poll within the planned instruction to monitor and determine learner progress. These are some popular digital quizzes:

- Quizlet
- Socrative
- Kahoot!
- Pear Deck
- Nearpod

The first three tools on the list, Quizlet, Socrative, and Kahoot!, function as simple closed-response assessments that measure basic learner recall of information. A benefit of using this technology-enabled formative assessment is that the school librarian can quickly access data on learner progress. These reports provide immediate feedback.

Pear Deck and Nearpod function in a similar way, though these assessment tools are embedded within learning content. In this way, assessment and learning become more integrated, and instruction has the potential to be more personalized.

ASSESSMENT IN ACTION
ELECTRONIC QUIZ

Seventh-grade learners have been using the school databases for inquiry. They will begin a project in which they will also use websites as an option for gathering their information. Prior lessons reviewed authority and bias. This lesson continues these ideas.

AASL Standards Framework for Learners

 VI.A.3. Learners follow ethical and legal guidelines for gathering and using information by evaluating information for accuracy, validity, social and cultural context, and appropriateness for need.

CCSS: English Language Arts–Literacy

W.7.8. Gather relevant information from multiple print and digital sources, using search terms effectively; assess the credibility and accuracy of each source; and quote or paraphrase the data and conclusions of others while avoiding plagiarism and following a standard format for citation.

The school librarian will model exploring different components of a website to check for authority (e.g., who wrote the information; what type of agency published or hosts the site) and credibility (e.g., what is the purpose of the site; how can information be verified) during a mini lesson on authority and credibility of online resources. The lesson will be delivered using a digital presentation such as PowerPoint or Loom and include opportunities for learner engagement and assessment with an embedded electronic quiz.

Using an embedded electronic assessment tool, school librarians can measure learners' progress during instruction. This method assesses learner understanding and engages learners during instruction. Assessing learner understanding in real time provides the school librarian with additional opportunity for teaching, if necessary, during the time of instruction.

Each of the preceding assessment tools relies on the use of a technology device. However, use of polls and quizzes is possible without technology. Paper-and-pencil quizzes with objective, closed responses can also be used. There has been a shift away from this method in recent years because this type of assessment takes a bit longer to gather and analyze results and is less environmentally friendly. However, paper and pencil could be an option when seeking alternatives to technology-heavy instruction or alternatives for differentiation for some learners requiring accommodations.

Conferences and Interviews

Discussion-based assessments can be used as formative assessments. These discussions often appear to be casual, but asking a learner how they are progressing or if they are in need of assistance will often yield a good deal of information on their progress. A more-formal interview or conference with each learner as they are working throughout an inquiry project will identify whether a learner is progressing or whether there is an area that may need clarification or assistance. This personalized formative assessment allows the school librarian to target individual learner questions and roadblocks and to offer individual assistance, as well as providing an opportunity for general clarification to a group of learners if common issues arise.

ASSESSMENT IN ACTION
CONFERENCING

Learners in an eleventh-grade earth science class are working on an inquiry unit. They are investigating the impact of natural hazards, climate change, or availability of natural resources and how these environmental factors impact human activity. The science educator and school librarian are both on hand to help guide the inquiry process once learners begin their independent investigation. As learners are working, the school librarian and the science educator conference with learners individually.

AASL Standards Framework for Learners

I.D.2. Learners participate in an ongoing inquiry-based process by engaging in sustained inquiry.

I.D.4. Learners participate in an ongoing inquiry-based process by using reflection to guide informed decisions.

V.D.3. Learners develop through experience and reflection by open-mindedly accepting feedback for positive and constructive growth.

NextGen Science Standard

HS-ESS3-1. Construct an explanation based on evidence for how the availability of natural resources, occurrence of natural hazards, and changes in climate have influenced human activity.

A conference is an effective assessment to use during a longer, sustained inquiry unit when learners have some discretion in selecting their topics and resources. Conferencing allows for individualized attention to each learner to check that they are making progress toward the learning goal. This assessment provides an opportunity for the learner to ask questions about challenges they may be facing. The conference allows the school librarian to provide targeted and personalized assistance.

Observation and Note Charts

A focused observation form or anecdotal note chart is a great tool to implement as learners work independently on an authentic learning task. This type of intentional observation assessment records what a learner is able to accomplish when tackling a real-life task, allowing further development of scaffolded activities and planning for consecutively challenging or remedial interventions that support future learning interactions. These notes ground teaching decisions and provide context for learner progress through everyday learning interactions.

When using observation or anecdotal notes, it is important to provide enough detail about the progress each learner is making in achieving the overall learning goal. To be most beneficial, a learning goal or objective should be stated, and then descriptive measures should be recorded for the learner. Also, whenever possible, capture concrete examples of how the learner is progressing toward meeting the learning goal. For example, while observing, if a learner is able to locate and use the school databases for information on an inquiry assignment, a note can be made to indicate that the learner has used, for example, PebbleGo for the assignment. This notation will help identify what has been accomplished and what skills can continue to be developed in later lessons. In this example, the goal may be to use a different database or a variety of databases within an inquiry project.

It is helpful if anecdotal notes are captured and recorded over time on one observation form (figure 3.1) that is easily shared with collaborating teaching peers and others who may also be working on similar skills with the learners. This type of data aids in the common discussion of learner progress.

Exit Tickets

An exit ticket can be an effective way to get immediate feedback on a lesson just after it occurs. This feedback can be used to help direct individual learners as well as provide direction for instruction. As with other formative assessments discussed in this chapter, exit tickets can be collected in a variety of ways, both with the aid of technology and without. For this reason, examples of exit tickets are discussed in three different formats: pen and paper, electronic (e.g., Padlet, Poll Everywhere, Google Forms), and video (e.g., Flip [formerly Flipgrid] or Seesaw).

Though the format and collection mechanism of an exit ticket may change, the intent remains consistent. An exit ticket is an assessment tool used to measure progress of learners toward meeting an identified skill or learning goal and is done at the close of a period of instruction. The exit ticket provides immediate feedback from the learner about their success in meeting a goal. It may also identify for the school librarian areas that require additional assistance or instruction.

Exit tickets begin with a prompt provided by the school librarian. This prompt can take a variety of formats, from very specific questions about a given instructional task (e.g., where are you in the inquiry task and what is your next step?) to more-general prompts (e.g., what was one thing that you struggled with during your work today?). The school librarian will be able to review the information shared

FIGURE 3.1
Example observation form

EDUCATOR NAME	Read the chapter titles with question in mind	Located the chapter/section that could provide an appropriate answer	Identified main topic in lead paragraph	Identified (highlighted) possible key words for further investigation
Date	Jan. 24	Jan. 24	Jan. 31 (Future lesson)	Jan. 31 (Future lesson)
Student A	X	X		
Student B	Required Assistance (RA)	RA		
Student C	X	RA		

and determine the best next steps. Before deploying an exit ticket, it is important to determine the purpose of this assessment. This knowledge will help determine the prompt as well as how the collected data can best be used. Potential goals for an exit ticket include preparation for instruction in the next learning session, identification of specific learners who may need additional assistance before they can progress to the next steps in the learning task, or identification of skills that were more globally challenging for a group of learners and will need revisiting in future lessons to work toward mastery.

Depending on the goal of the exit ticket, the school librarian can use the responses to support learners or make note of materials that have not yet been mastered by a particular group or set of learners and will need to be reviewed in another learning experience. One key is to make sure the questions are purposeful. They should measure learner understanding, not just create busy work or ask learners to demonstrate shallow understanding that does not drive future instruction.

ASSESSMENT IN ACTION
EXIT TICKET

The school librarian encourages second-grade learners to consider on-level books to read during independent reading time. A lesson will focus on how learners can determine books of interest, as well as books that support reading fluency and comprehension and understanding at grade level. The librarian will model locating books in the school library based on interest and strategies for determining if a book can be read independently. Learners will use a touch exit ticket (e.g., a large poster board, a touch screen) to evaluate their success in locating a book.

AASL Standards Framework for Learners

 V.A.1. Learners develop and satisfy personal curiosity by reading widely and deeply in multiple formats and write and create for a variety of purposes.

CCSS: English Language Arts–Literacy

RF.2.3. Know and apply grade-level phonics and word analysis skills in decoding words.

RF.2.4. Read with sufficient accuracy and fluency to support comprehension.

Learners will have the opportunity to explore and select books they want to read independently. The school librarian will suggest and model strategies to consider during selection:

» Look at the cover and the title.
» Read the description on the back of the book.
» Scan the text (consider the font size, white space).
» Look at the illustrations.
» Check the number of pages.
» Try the five-finger test. (This assessment asks learners to select a random page in a book and begin reading. They will raise one finger each time they encounter a word they don't know or cannot read. If they have raised five fingers before getting to the end of the page, the book may be challenging for their reading level.)

Everyone will check out a book. As learners exit the school library, they will be asked to complete the touch exit ticket. Learners will select one of the following answers on a large poster:

1. I found a book I am excited to read; I can read it.
2. I found a book I think I will like; some of the words feel a little tricky.
3. I found a book that is easy to read; I am not sure if I will like it.
4. I have a book; I might want to exchange it before our next library class.

The exit ticket allows the school librarian to help learners identify books better aligned with their interest or reading level or to monitor those who may need further assistance with reading advisory.

Electronic exit tickets have the same function as pencil-and-paper assessments. One benefit of using an electronic format is that data can be collected, analyzed, and stored. These data can further be shared with any collaborating teaching peers. Tools such as Padlet also allow for sharing among learners (either publicly or anonymously) to provide a platform for instructional discussion among learners.

Video assessments can be used to demonstrate learning through a recorded response to the provided prompt. This type of assessment tool can be used to diversify learner engagement and allow for more variety in the way learners authentically give voice to their learning experience. Video assessments can also be easily shared with others within and among the education community.

Graphic Organizers

Graphic organizers are assessment tools that allow learners to visually represent their progress toward meeting learning goals. These tools provide structure and space for learners to document their ideas as they progress through a critical-thinking process. These organizers visually map out the mental path a learner takes as they progress through a given learning task.

Graphic organizers commonly used in a school library can take several forms:

- Idea webs
- Diagrams, charts, and matrices
- Planning or organizing documents

Idea webs are useful for processing relationship information. These tools are often used during the beginning stages of inquiry to help learners develop questions, consider information relationships, and determine a primary focus for investigation. Idea webs begin with a broad idea and allow learners to brainstorm and make connections to ideas they already have about a given topic. These ideas can be presented in words, phrases, or even pictures. Idea webs are similar to the concept maps used as diagnostic assessments in chapter 2, but here they are used to direct learner understanding toward building and creating these connections.

Charts, matrices, diagrams, and planning documents provide a structure for learners to organize their thinking throughout the learning process. Charts build on data literacy skills that help develop good users of numeric information. These types of visual organizers allow learners to document their understanding of the learning process when working with concepts in the areas of computational data, scientific data, and problem solving. Diagrams may show relational data. A Venn diagram, for instance, visually demonstrates comparisons of information. A planning document or organizer can provide learners with a workspace to document and synthesize new understanding.

Graphic organizers are generally created by the school librarian prior to instruction. These tools may be specific to a learning task or more general to be used to structure and guide the inquiry process. Figure 3.2 shows an example of a graphic organizer that can be adapted. A graphic organizer used as an assessment tool more specifically aligned with an inquiry lesson is demonstrated here. Though the example is general, it can be revised and tailored to document specific learning tasks for the content addressed in a lesson.

FIGURE 3.2
General graphic organizer

Five interesting facts I want to share:

Two questions I thought of as I read:	Why I picked this topic to explore:

Where I found my information today:

Group or Collaborative Assessments

Learners can work together to demonstrate the new understanding they have gained about content or the inquiry process. This type of assessment allows learners to give voice to their progress and demonstrate their success, as well as challenges, in an authentic manner. Group or collaborative peer-to-peer assessment may take several forms:

- Signaling and dipstick assessments
- Chalk talks and gallery walks
- Partner share (organized with specific or informal prompts)

Often, it can be beneficial to assess how the entire class is progressing throughout a lesson. Dipstick assessments provide an opportunity to check learner understanding at a given point in time. They are developed to be quick and simple. Learners may be given a simple tool, such as a happy/sad face or a red/green two-sided card, with which they can easily respond to simple yes/no questions. This assessment task requires the group of learners to signal a response that the school librarian can then visually scan to measure group understanding. Examples of these signaling or dipstick assessments include a thumbs-up/thumbs-down response or display of fingers in response to a verbal question or statement (e.g., in response to "show me how many characters were present in the book," learners raise the correct number of fingers to demonstrate understanding of character). Although often a quick means of formative assessment, dipstick assessments can be difficult to track and are rarely the only means of assessment used in a lesson. Other peer assessments provide a similar group check in a more-formalized approach.

Participatory learning is a cornerstone of instruction in the school library. Use of chalk talks and gallery walks dictates that learners will share their ongoing learning, engage in discussion about the learning, and have an opportunity to ask and answer questions about the learning process. Through this method of formative assessment, learners can get authentic feedback from others in the class. The learner who shared the material can authentically share their own work, starting a scholarly conversation. Other learners can ask clarifying questions, make comments or suggestions, and engage in the discussion with the author.

Gallery walks and chalk talks can be done verbally, where there is opportunity for open discussion and dialogue. These activities can also be done more introspectively, allowing learners to contemplate ideas and then leave comments and questions on a written document for the author to review later. A traditional gallery walk is conducted in person with written artifacts. However, this activity and assessment can be modified for a virtual environment, using videoconferencing technology or shared documents, or both.

ASSESSMENT IN ACTION
GALLERY WALK

Fourth-grade learners are examining images for visual literacy cues and translating their discoveries into textual elements. In this lesson, the school librarian asks the learners to work with a partner to analyze a picture for information. A gallery walk is used to assess learner understanding of visual literacy cues.

AASL Standards Framework for Learners

III.B.1. Learners participate in personal, social, and intellectual networks by using a variety of communication tools and resources.
III.B.2. Learners participate in personal, social, and intellectual networks by establishing connections with other learners to build on their own prior knowledge and create new knowledge.

CCSS: English Language Arts–Literacy

W.4.9. Draw evidence from literary or informational texts to support analysis, reflection, and research.

Pictures or diagrams are placed on large note sheets (or chart paper), each on a different table throughout the room. Small learner groups are invited to complete a gallery walk around each table, pausing for three to five minutes at each picture for discussion. Learners then add comments or information about the pictures to the chart paper as they explore the different images. The school librarian can walk among groups to provide assistance and prompt further input to help capture the discussion.

Engaging in a gallery walk with a partner allows learners the opportunity to explore and analyze visual cues by examining a picture from multiple perspectives. Through collaborative exploration of multiple images, learners share insights with their partner and begin to make new connections with the visual information. Learners build on their own knowledge and the knowledge of others to confirm or create new understanding of the information presented.

Partner or group shared assessment allows insight into each learner's progress through the conversations shared between learners. Using these strategies, learners provide feedback about their learning and understanding with a peer. These active learning assessments may be combined with school librarian observation and note cards.

Partner or shared assessment is one effective way to ensure that all learners are engaged and have an opportunity to voice their understanding. In traditional direct instruction, a classroom educator or school librarian may ask a question and rely on one learner to respond (usually after being called on, with raised hand). This activity limits the engagement of learning to one-to-one between the educator and the one learner selected to respond. Use of partner assessment such as a think-pair-share activity allows *every* learner to participate and share their response within their group. The school librarian can monitor these responses and redirect or summarize as needed once all learners have participated.

ASSESSMENT IN ACTION
THINK-PAIR-SHARE

Learners in second grade focus on community and civics as a theme throughout the year. In a read-aloud lesson, the school librarian engages learners in prediction and connection by asking learners to share with a shoulder partner (a learner seated next to them) their personal experiences related to events in the story and ideas predicting what may happen next for the characters in the story.

AASL Standards Framework for Learners

 III.C.1. Learners work productively with others to solve problems by soliciting and responding to feedback from others.

C3 Framework for Social Studies State Standards

D2.Civ.9.K-2. Follow agreed-upon rules for discussions while responding attentively to others when addressing ideas and making decisions as a group.

The use of a think-pair-share assessment allows each learner the opportunity to consider and express their ideas while also presenting the opportunity to engage in discussion-based protocol. Once the learners have had a short time to share among themselves, a few groups are invited to share their prediction ideas with the whole class. This activity allows the school librarian an opportunity to monitor understanding and redirect instruction, if needed.

For a more deeply engaged peer experience, the discussion may be more formalized. In this assessment approach, the prompt should be specific to the learning task. TAG is an example of a more-formalized, discussion-type of partner assessment. TAG is an acronym for the prompts that may be suggested when employing this assessment model:

- **T**ell your peer something about your learning progress.
- **A**sk a thoughtful question.
- **G**ive positive suggestions/feedback.

This strategy, in which learners must articulate their progress or provide feedback about their understanding, allows for social engagement as well as critical thinking in the learning process. TAG assessment feedback will likely include a discussion about the specific learning task. It is helpful to model this feedback for and with learners as they build their ability to engage with their peers in academic dialogue.

Assessing Collaborative Skills

Personal growth and what are often described as "soft skills" within the AASL Standards affective Domain Share are frequently mentioned as desired traits as learners prepare to engage within the global community. Preparation for lifelong learning and college and career remains at the forefront to meet the Competencies in the *AASL Standards Framework for Learners* (AASL 2018a). Collaboration is therefore one of the six Shared Foundations within the AASL Standards framework. Not only does collaboration enhance individual achievement and accountability, but it also fosters better intergroup relations to assist with reducing prejudice and increasing acceptance of others (Meyers 2008).

Effective school libraries foster participatory learning experiences. It is necessary that school librarians have a plan to assess these collaborative learner interactions. Using a modification of Mueller's (2009) Collaborative Framework, collaboration assessments may consider the following four categories:

1. Participation in and contribution to group tasks
2. Understanding and knowledge of task or skill
3. Effective group functioning and relationships
4. Communication

Collaboration is frequently assessed at the group level. The school librarian assesses how well the group understands and demonstrates skills as learners progress together. Collaboration is often assessed through observation of learners participating in a group task. Assessment of collaboration can become tricky when trying to balance a fair and equitable means to determine individual learning and group productivity. Remembering that collaboration does not always take place where it can be observed, multiple opportunities for assessment should be established. These methods could include self-assessment and peer assessment in addition to observations.

Setting expectations for collaborative learning is beneficial. One assessment strategy for collaboration might include the use of contracts. Before starting an extensive project that includes multiple learners working together, learners should be made aware of the roles, responsibilities, and expectations for each member. A contract may outline how each person is responsible for research, learning, planning, and the like. Use of a graphic organizer may also work well. This tool allows for a visual representation of expectations and provides a means to record how individuals are contributing. Other options include creating a checklist of expectations. Such a checklist may be developed using the following exemplars and adding the specific tasks of a given assignment:

- Performs fair share of the work
- Asks questions and engages in discussion
- Follows agreed-upon procedures
- Avoids disruptive or off-task behavior
- Openly considers the ideas and perspectives of others
- Guides group toward agreement, consensus, or compromise
- Makes eye contact and does not interrupt speaker
- Listens respectfully and objectively

Collaboration must be taught. Use of electronic collaborative tools may help embed strategies with which learners already feel comfortable within the teaching and learning space of the school library. Google Workspace (formerly G Suite), Prezi, Smore for Teams, and some Microsoft tools all allow learners to share and exchange work. Additionally, these tools will often create a record of the learner contribution process.

ASSESSMENT IN ACTION
VIRTUAL POSTER

Ninth-grade learners are working collaboratively to contribute to a virtual poster. The poster will display multiple resources and information about a health topic of the learners' choice. The group may decide on the final topic, but information must be presented that highlights and credits multiple viewpoints.

AASL Standards Framework for Learners

 II.C.2. Learners exhibit empathy with and tolerance for diverse ideas by contributing to discussions in which multiple viewpoints on a topic are expressed.

 IV.C.2. Learners exchange information resources within and beyond their learning community by contributing to collaboratively constructed information sites by ethically using and reproducing others' work.

ISTE Standards for Students

Creative Communicator 1.6. Students communicate clearly and express themselves creatively for a variety of purposes using the platforms, tools, styles, formats, and digital media appropriate to their goals.

Global Collaborator 1.7. Students use digital tools to broaden their perspectives and enrich their learning by collaborating with others and working effectively in teams locally and globally.

A shared product requires that the group thoroughly research the ethical considerations as well as demonstrate empathy toward any varying positions. The virtual poster must include links to reliable sources along with attribution to these resources. The poster should also be visually appealing and include some static facts and information.

A virtual poster allows multiple contributors to add content to demonstrate their understanding. This product documents a collective means to assess learner progress in documenting digital resources. The poster also allows the school librarian to evaluate the negotiated learning experience of a group of learners because the product documents the perspective of more than one individual.

Reflection as Assessment

Reflection provides an opportunity for learners to focus on their progress toward mastery. This approach is most effective when reflection has been previously modeled. Reflective assessment should guide learners away from a general summary of their product and toward their understanding and application of their learning process. Good reflections discuss what the student learned and how this learning can be applied in the future, as well as what they may do differently in later projects. With collaborative work, the reflection should clearly outline the learner's role within the group rather than the lack of work of others.

Use of reflection is also a great way for school librarians to modify activities for future use. After analyzing learner views on a project, the school librarian is able to identify learner perceptions of success. When done well, reflections often identify challenges that learners encountered. These common challenges can then be used by school librarians to clarify assignment expectations, scaffold learning, and make adjustments to instruction for future success with a project or idea.

Learning logs are a specific type of reflective assessment tool. This assessment provides an opportunity for learners to document their thinking throughout the learning while identifying their problem-solving process (see also "Learning Logs" in chapter 4). Learning logs can be open, allowing learners to document their inquiry journey in their own words without a set structure. This format could include bulleted lists of discoveries, learner questions, and reflective thoughts on the inquiry process, as well as information findings. These logs may be useful over time to provide open reflection for learners who have worked with this tool. Learning logs can also be guided, as in the figure 3.3 example on the following page, whereby learners respond to questions or prompts throughout the learning process to help guide them to the next stage of their inquiry experience.

Reflection can take place throughout the learning process. It can be in-depth or short, depending on other types of assessment being used.

FIGURE 3.3

Example guided learning log

Think about the following and record your responses as you investigate your topic.

1. Important ideas I want to remember:

_____

_____

_____

2. How do these ideas relate to my own life?

_____

_____

_____

3. How does this topic relate to other things I have read or learned?

_____

_____

_____

4. What is something I am having trouble understanding? What do I want to ask for help with?

_____

_____

_____

_____

Summative Assessments

Summative assessments document a learner's progress throughout a learning experience or instructional unit. This assessment is often reflected in a final grade or feedback to the learner that documents understanding or demonstration of mastery of a skill or concept. Summative assessments are frequently the final learning project or product. An assessment tool is used to determine or document achievement of culminating goals and objectives. In the school library, it is best when these projects or products are performance-based and integrate demonstration of content curriculum knowledge as well as library and information skills and inquiry tasks. Inclusion of library skills in the summative assessment process of a learning lesson or series aids the school librarian in determining what information was retained and mastered as well as whether there is a need to develop further teaching or materials related to the objectives.

Common Summative Assessments Used

In this chapter we will explore common summative assessments used in the school library. These tools may be developed and integrated with content skills and used to assess learning together with the content-area teaching peer. They also may be used independently to assess learning that has taken place in the school library and that supports other academic achievements. Summative assessments may be developed and used collaboratively with a teaching peer to assess both content and library skills or developed independently and used only by the school librarian. School library summative assessments can take several forms:

- Rubrics
- Learning logs
- Portfolios

Rubrics

Rubrics clarify expectations of an assignment for the learner. This clarification allows the learner some ownership of the work while also providing direct guidance on the part of the school librarian. There is also an opportunity to integrate collaborative content instruction by developing one overall rubric for an assignment that is conducted under the coordination of a school librarian and a classroom educator. Rubrics present an evaluative "range" for performance quality that learners can identify and strive for. A rubric begins with the task definition—the instructions for the assignment—followed by a grid of rows and columns. Each row will specify the knowledge, skills, or behavior the learner is expected to demonstrate. Finally, each column will describe a level of mastery or scale of proficiency for the task.

TIPS FOR CREATING A WELL-DEVELOPED RUBRIC

» **Clearly identify what is being assessed.** Do not include "extra" rows unless there has been some instruction on the expectations for these skills.

» **Identify the levels of mastery (columns).** It is ideal to have four columns. Columns can be labeled in a variety of ways (e.g., Exemplary/Meeting Expectations/Approaching/Not Meeting Expectations; 1/2/3/4; Advanced/Satisfactory/Developing/Unacceptable). Having an even number ensures that the middle does not become a "default" selection.

» **Define the characteristics for each cell.** Consider the scoring criteria for each category. If partial credit may be earned in any cell, be sure you have a means to communicate this feedback to learners (you might want to highlight or circle parts of the cell or provide written feedback as well as award partial points). Each cell should have different characteristics. Careful scoring and learner feedback allow learners to understand where they have met expectations and where they still have areas to grow.

» **Use observable, measurable language.** When developing the criteria for each cell of the rubric, be sure that the items being assessed can be objectively measured.

It is important that criteria clearly differentiate one performance level from the next. One benefit of using a rubric is the ability to assess learners consistently from learner to learner. Finally, a rubric can be created *with* the learners. When learners are engaged in rubric creation, they can be more vested in and accountable for the expectations of the assignment. Although rubrics are created to guide the learner and aid in evaluating the learning process, the use of a rubric during and at the end of a lesson demonstrates how the rubric can be used by both the school librarian and learner to measure learning in the school library.

ASSESSMENT IN ACTION
RUBRIC

Fifth-grade learners are working on scientific discovery. They will host a science fair to showcase their understanding of the design process in the upcoming months. In preparation, each learner selects a topic of interest to investigate and will have opportunities to visit the school library maker lab. A rubric is developed to guide the learners' investigation and experimentation.

AASL Standards Framework for Learners

V.B.1. Learners construct new knowledge by problem solving through cycles of design, implementation, and reflection.
V.B.2. Learners construct new knowledge by persisting through self-directed pursuits by tinkering and making.

NextGen Science Standards

5-PS1. Planning and Carrying Out Investigations: Conduct an investigation collaboratively to produce data to serve as the basis for evidence, using fair tests in which variables are controlled and the number of trials considered.

CCSS: English Language Arts–Literacy

W.5.9. Draw evidence from literary or informational texts to support analysis, reflection, and research.

A detailed rubric of required elements is provided for each learner to address during the investigation of their topic and throughout the construction of an experimental design. Every learner must provide findings of their investigation, documented using a standardized format that is outlined in the written rubric. The classroom educator, as well as the school librarian, is available to guide learners in their information investigation and in the final implementation stages of the project. Everyone uses the rubric to ensure that all steps are followed and to communicate the expectations for success.

Learning Logs

Learning logs can assess how learners progressed at various points in the learning process. Through this measure, learners reflect on and share their learning in written format. Using a learning log, learners record their process, note new understanding, identify questions that arose through their discovery, and make connections to new understandings. Learners can use a learning log to document their learning process (see "Reflection as Assessment" in chapter 3). This log can function as a formative assessment as learning occurs, presenting an opportunity to redirect learning if needed. When the log is submitted at the conclusion of a project, it is used to demonstrate final learning results and as a summative assessment. The learning log can be completed in analog form or in a digital environment, allowing for this tool to be adapted to the virtual space.

Portfolio

A portfolio, whether curated electronically or in print, is a purposeful collection of a learner's work. This assessment tool provides an opportunity for learners to demonstrate and reflect on their learning. It is also an opportunity for the school librarian, as well as a potential additional audience, to assess each learner's mastery of content based on evidence selected and provided. A portfolio is often a multimedia presentation, though it may remain text-based. Using artifacts, or examples of selected evidence of learning, a student learner documents their learning experience. There is nearly always a reflection component to a portfolio that includes the learner's description of their learning journey or process.

5

Learner Self-Assessments

Self-assessment is an important consideration for learner growth and development. The benefits of self-assessment are shared throughout the *National School Library Standards*. Personal growth and development naturally align with the ideals of self-assessment. Learners from a young age can be guided through the process of monitoring and evaluating their progress in learning. The assessment process of learners is often scaffolded to include supportive tools and strategies for learners to self-assess, along with the school librarian's use of formative assessment tools such as graphic organizers to facilitate learner development of organization and accountability. With practice, learners may be able to articulate their self-assessment process or perform the stages of assessment, when properly modeled and developed, through a less structured format.

Self-assessment can be just as effective as any other form of assessment in guiding learners in their growth and understanding of new information. However, for the method to be effective, learners must learn how to self-assess effectively. This learning typically means the school librarian must model and demonstrate assessment and allow time for learner practice. One way to begin the use of self-assessment is to use formative assessment that provides learner feedback. This strategy shows learners how to monitor ongoing learning behaviors and ways to redirect learning when they encounter challenges. Modeling and feedback should explicitly include self-talk and reflection.

This chapter identifies self-assessment in two parts: early self-assessment that is introductory and can be used almost immediately, and later self-assessment that progresses to more-advanced methods, which should be used after some practice and scaffolding have occurred to demonstrate how learners may be most successful.

Early Self-Assessment Strategies

Early self-assessment strategies are commonly used as a means for learners to communicate with the school librarian. This information may include notification that the learner is in need of assistance as they work independently through assigned tasks or an alert regarding progress as instruction takes place. It can also be a way to assess progress or participate during and after a lesson. Though these are examples and may have variations, I will highlight several popular self-assessments that can be used as stand-alone assessments for a lesson or within a lesson to allow learners to gauge their progress toward meeting lesson objectives:

- Parking lot
- Colored stacking cups or cards
- Social media "post"
- Signaling

Parking Lot

Inviting learners to provide feedback while working or at the end of a lesson can be a great way to obtain learner feedback. Notes, comments, or sticky pads are all good options for collecting feedback. Learners can provide input about where they are feeling confident and where they need added support in a given lesson. You can gather this information through a parking lot approach whereby learners are invited to place comments and notes with questions in designated areas as they require assistance. Hosting a parking lot, or a discussion board or chat space in a virtual setting, provides a space for learners to post questions or wonderings that they feel confident will be addressed and allows them to continue working until they get assistance.

The parking lot may be separated into different types of space, or categories, or it may be spread out into different areas of the room to address different needs, depending on the context of the project. One area may be for those learners who require assistance before they are able to go further in their work (e.g., "I am stuck locating information on my topic") whereas another area may be for issues that can be addressed in a small group (e.g., "I would like to review creating citations for a website"). By allowing learners to post their concerns through comments in a parking lot, the school librarian is able to group like issues and address those that are of more-immediate concern to best help all learners progress through their work.

Colored Stacking Cups or Cards

Use of colored cups or cards during independent work allows the learner to communicate their progress and nonverbally signal any need for assistance. For this assessment strategy, each learner is provided a complete set of cups or cards—green, yellow, and red—at the onset of the lesson. Once independent work begins, the learner sets out the appropriate cup or card to indicate their level of comfort with the lesson:

- green = all set, no assistance needed
- yellow = have questions, but can continue working for now
- red = need immediate assistance, work cannot progress

This technique allows the school librarian and educator partners to visually assess which learners need assistance. The school librarian may even decide to regroup learners with common needs. This assessment tool can be further modified with specific instructions such as "place your yellow card on your desk if you need assistance with citations" if adequate assistance is available, and small groups can easily be created for guided instruction.

Social Media "Post"

Engaging learners in self-assessment that mirrors everyday activities is important and can be an effective means of self-assessment. Relatable self-assessments allow learners to demonstrate or express their understanding while also practicing activities that are authentic representations of skills that transfer into their nonacademic lives. One way to introduce authentic practice is through information creation.

SELFIE AS AN ACRONYM FOR SELF-ASSESSMENT

Allow learners to capture a photo of their work and share it online, using the acronym SELFIE to promote expectations for learners to self-assess the work they post. This example of the SELFIE acronym is designed for use with mathematics:

- » **S**howed my work
- » **E**xplained my answers
- » **L**ots of math vocabulary used
- » **F**ound multiple solutions
- » **I** persevered through the problem
- » **E**liminated careless errors

Assessment practices that mimic the sharing of information that learners will participate in beyond the academic setting help prepare them for engagement in a global community. When possible, ask learners to share their work through this self-expression. Learners are then building life skills while also assessing their own progress in the learning process of meeting the lesson objective.

ASSESSMENT IN ACTION
TWEET SELF-ASSESSMENT

Sixth-grade learners are beginning an inquiry investigation using both print and electronic resources in the school library over several weeks. Learners will be required to submit a bibliography of the resources they use throughout their investigation. The school librarian provides a lesson on citation of web resources. To self-assess understanding of citation, learners will "tweet" their understanding of online citation rules.

AASL Standards Framework for Learners

 VI.B.1. Learners use valid information and reasoned conclusions to make ethical decisions in the creation of knowledge by ethically using and reproducing others' work.

VI.B.2. Learners use valid information and reasoned conclusions to make ethical decisions in the creation of knowledge by acknowledging authorship and demonstrating respect for the intellectual property of others.

ISTE Standards for Students

Digital Citizen 1.2. Students recognize the rights, responsibilities, and opportunities of living, learning, and working in an interconnected digital world, and they act and model in ways that are safe, legal and ethical.

Citation of online resources can get tricky. Attribution can be complex when authorship is not always available or when different types of resources are used. To self-assess their understanding, learners will be asked to tweet a brief description of their understanding. They will be provided the following instruction:

» Describe today's lesson in 140 characters; give the lesson a hashtag (e.g., #trickywebcitation)

And a few prompts, such as these:

» Describe the format you should use for a website (with or without author) citation.

» Tweet one "irregular" or "tricky" rule to watch out for.

» Describe the information that should always be included in a web-site citation.

» Describe what information to include when using images from a website.

These tweets will be reviewed by the school librarian, and any incorrect content can then be reviewed with the class. The tweets will also be shared on an electronic bulletin board as visual reminders throughout the unit.

Signaling

A school librarian can quickly assess understanding by incorporating silent signals into a lesson. This type of assessment asks learners to visually demonstrate their perceived understanding of material by raising their hands. This feedback allows the school librarian to modify or adjust instruction based on learner responses. Signals can be used in both virtual and face-to-face lessons, using physical hand signs as well as virtual reactions in an online space. Signals help monitor the understanding of an entire set of learners through a quick, visual scan. A chart of ideas for use of signals is included in figure 5.1.

FIGURE 5.1

Chart of signals used for formative self-assessment

I agree/yes

I disagree/no

Me too/ I relate to that

True

I want to add a counterpoint

I want to add to the discussion

I need to use the restroom

Later Self-Assessment Strategies

After self-assessment has been introduced and practiced, more-complex tools can be implemented. Learners are now ready to engage with self-monitored progress in their learning. This step places significant learner ownership in the assessment process. The following self-assessments work best after some instruction on self-assessment:

- Checklists
- Journaling
- Rating scales
- Reflection

Checklists

Checklists usually offer a clear, objective format that learners can use to align their own work to the expectations of the assignment (figure 5.2). They can be used while a task is in process or at the completion of an assignment. A *yes/no* or *check if complete* format works best. However, learners must critically evaluate their progress and assess how their learning and understanding are moving toward meeting the lesson objectives. The learner may need to be able to evaluate key points in the process for which they will need to engage the assistance of the school librarian. It can be helpful for the school librarian to create, or review in detail, each step of the checklist with the learners, especially if the expectations of the checklist are new. If the checklist is to be a useful assessment tool, the learner must be able to effectively use it to measure their own progress. For this reason, it is recommended to create a checklist with very discrete tasks for evaluation. Having smaller steps to evaluate can make self-assessment more meaningful.

Journaling

Journals provide access into the learner's thinking process. They allow descriptive feedback and reflection that address the learner's progress through a task. Writing prompts may be required to elicit responses that demonstrate learner understanding. If using prompts, designing prompts that require some type of learner synthesis and demonstration of understanding is key. Such responses will allow the school librarian to assess the learner in meeting lesson objectives. Young learners or learners who are not reading and writing at grade level may require sentence starters or be allowed to include pictures in their journal. Learners can also ask questions and seek guidance on how they can best progress through an assignment. For this reason, it can be helpful to include prompts that ask learners if they need help or are having difficulty with an assigned task.

FIGURE 5.2

Example checklist

PURPOSE AND PERSPECTIVE		
• Is the main purpose to inform rather than to try to sell me something?	Y	N
• Does the site present information without trying to sway my opinion?	Y	N
• Does the site present all sides of the issue in an objective way?	Y	N

AUTHORITY		
• Can I find the author of the site?	Y	N
• Does the author/organization have a good reputation?	Y	N
• Is the author a known expert?	Y	N

ACCURACY		
• Is the information correct?	Y	N
• Can the information be verified?	Y	N
• Do other sites have similar information or confirm this information?	Y	N

READABILITY		
• Do I understand the information on the site without relying on other sources?	Y	N

TIMELINESS		
• Does the site have a date that it was created?	Y	N
• Is the date recent?	Y	N

LINKS		
• Do the links within the site take me to good websites? Do the links work?	Y	N
• Does the website have an owner (e.g., .org [nonprofit], .edu [education], .gov [government])?	Y	N

SAMPLE JOURNAL PROMPTS

» What was the most difficult part of the assignment (project, task), and why was it challenging? What did you do to overcome this challenge?

» What were three things you accomplished during the project? Explain how you can use these tasks in a future research project.

» How did you evaluate the resources you used for your paper/project? How do you know these sources are reliable?

» Do you require assistance at this point in your project? What help or resources do you need to be successful?

Rating Scales

Rating scales are assessment tools used by learners that state specific criteria related to the stated lesson objective. Scales allow the learner to determine if they are making progress toward the intended outcome or if they may need redirection, additional guidance, or assistance. For this tool to be effective, it is essential that the language and descriptors used are clear and specific. This assessment tool can be particularly helpful when learners are attempting to set goals or demonstrate progress over time. Descriptive frequency indicators such as Always/Sometimes/Never help learners assess areas of strength and areas to develop. Rating scales can have added impact by including items that require more than a simple rating (e.g., circle the skill that is most challenging for you).

Reflection

Reflection can be used to document learner progress as a self-assessment strategy. Learner reflections can then be shared with the school librarian to highlight any areas that may require assistance. Figure 5.3 shows an example of a short reflective exit ticket that can be completed to self-assess learner progression in an electronic format.

FIGURE 5.3
Reflection self-assessment

1. I was able to find information about my topic today.
    o Disagree
    o Somewhat
    o Agree

2. Using the checklist, I think my sources are good and my information is reliable and accurate.
    Not sure   1   2   3   4   5   Very Confident

3. I am still having trouble with one or more parts of my research. I have a question about:

_____

_____

_____

_____

_____

_____

_____

_____

6

Virtual Assessments

Learning in a virtual environment can present unique opportunities and challenges. Whether presenting materials synchronously, while learners are present in a learning platform, or asynchronously, whereby learners view, learn, and practice in their own time and space, it is essential that the school librarian continue to monitor learner growth and understanding in this space. Some assessment strategies that work well in person can be equally effective in this virtual environment. Other times, a different, unique approach must be considered to ensure learner achievement.

Teaching and Learning in an Online Setting

Virtual learning is just that—teaching and learning that occurs in an online space. Therefore, all the components and best practices of good instruction must also be present, including the assessment of learners. Formative assessment strategies are still required to monitor learner understanding and to inform instruction. It is not as easy to observe learner work and hold casual conversations when teaching in a digital space. Engaging multiple learners can be more challenging, as are opportunities to incorporate collaborative sharing and partner work. For these reasons, the use of multiple formative assessments within a lesson can allow for a *better* learning experience for both the learner and the school librarian.

Take advantage of the features, often available on online conferencing platforms, that mimic quick-check formative assessments deployed during in-person instruction. Not only does using these features (figure 6.1) allow the school librarian to monitor understanding throughout the progression of the lesson, but it also helps maintain engagement of the learner in a remote setting. Through varied and

FIGURE 6.1

Online instruction reactions

frequent formative assessment checks, the learner has the opportunity to demonstrate understanding of materials presented. These assessment measures also allow the school librarian to calibrate the instruction and make adjustments where needed.

Although it may seem intuitive to embed multiple technology-enabled assessment strategies, technology-enabled assessments are only one form of assessment that can be used in virtual instruction. At times, technology-free assessments may be better suited for the given task. Though instruction is taking place online, assessment is carried out offline. Learner assessment can take place through submission of learning artifacts, and learner progress is then determined through more-traditional assessment tasks.

Technology-Based Assessments

Many assessment strategies can be applied to learning using technology-based tools and implemented during face-to-face or virtual instruction. Several of the formative assessment strategies discussed in chapter 4 can be implemented through technology-embedded software. When used in the school library in a face-to-face setting, this software provides a few notable benefits. For learners, depending on the technology tool used and how the assessment is set up, it can provide complete anonymity for their response, which can promote honest feedback from anxious learners. Technology-based assessment also allows for near-instant feedback to the school librarian, and the technology tool frequently does at least some descriptive analysis of the results, which can be extremely helpful when you want to quickly assess the class in aggregate. Such data allow the school librarian to immediately determine learner strengths and weaknesses in knowledge and skills. Use of embedded technology assessments can occur and be beneficial in both an online and a face-to-face instruction format.

ASSESSMENT IN ACTION
ONLINE CONFERENCING POLL

In a ninth-grade hybrid classroom setting where some learners are present in the school library and some are joining the instruction remotely, the school librarian provides an introduction to different types of resources for an inquiry project. To assess learner knowledge of primary versus secondary resources, a conferencing poll is deployed whereby all learners can respond, both those in the room and those at a distance.

AASL Standards Framework for Learners

 I.A.2. Learners display curiosity and initiative by recalling prior and background knowledge as context for new meaning.

 IV.A.2. Learners act on an information need by identifying possible sources of information.

C3 Framework for Social Studies Standards

D1.5.9-12. Determine the kinds of sources that will be helpful in answering compelling and supporting questions, taking into consideration multiple points of view represented in the sources, the types of sources available, and the potential uses of the sources.

A poll can be used to capture learners' current understanding of primary and secondary sources for those participating in the physical space and those online. To electronically capture results for learners in both learning spaces:

» all learners would need to log on to the online learning platform to complete the poll, *or*

» a link to a poll generated from a polling platform external to the primary online learning platform would need to be shared with all learners, *or*

» separate polling systems would need to be used to account for responses in both settings (i.e., an electronic poll for remote learners, and either paper responses or raised hands for learners responding to poll questions in the physical space).

A poll deployed during hybrid instruction enables users in both formats to demonstrate their understanding of questions asked. If all learners have access to the Internet, a quick analysis of the results can be gathered for both groups. If not, those in the physical room can respond in an analog format while those online react to the poll. The school librarian can still use answers to gauge understanding and guide discussion based on results.

Technology-enhanced assessments require learners to interact with materials in ways that may be different from traditional pencil-and-paper formats. This strategy increases a learner's digital literacy skills and provides an opportunity for authentic engagement with tasks the learner may encounter outside an academic setting. As society relies more on automated activities (e.g., the Department of Motor Vehicles is using online assessments, everyday banking and shopping are increasingly moving online, and college and career applications and many common personal and household services are conducted in an online setting), familiarity with digital engagement benefits all learners.

CONCLUSION
Learner Assessment Used as Advocacy

Though school librarians do not usually maintain grades or grade books to document learner progress toward mastery, they do collect data about the individual progress and achievement of each learner in the school. This information can be shared with teaching peers, administrators, and decision makers to demonstrate how the school library impacts student achievement. In this way, learner assessment in the school library can be a key advocacy tool for school librarians to communicate learner progress to others in the education community.

Use of Assessment to Facilitate Stakeholder Conversations

School librarians continue to face antiquated stereotypes. These stereotypes are perpetuated by other members of the education community who do not have a clear understanding of the role that school librarians play in student learning and achievement. Lack of understanding of the instructional role of the school librarian exists among administrators and teaching peers as well as other decision makers and community members. Therefore, assessment practices and the purpose of assessment in the school library are commonly misunderstood.

This misunderstanding can be mitigated when sharing data on learner progress in key learning areas. The best way to share learner progress that occurs in the school library is to make learner growth and instructional practice transparent. Results of many of the assessment practices and tools discussed throughout this book can easily be shared with others in the school with this purpose in mind.

Some assessment data can be shared electronically as learners engage with material. For instance, if a Google Form is used by the school librarian as a means of formative assessment, the results can be shared via a link to a data spreadsheet. This data sharing allows other collaborators, such as the classroom educator, to add information, ask questions, and enter observations. These shared results could then become a powerful shared data resource used to document learner progress and growth among a teaching team. Such a data resource also functions as a documentation aid for conversations with administrators and school librarian evaluators.

Data sharing cannot be sporadic. It should be intentional and consistent if it is going to aid in conversations about student achievement and school library impact. For collected assessment data to be used successfully, information must be updated regularly. The school librarian should establish a regular cycle of data review with other educators and administrators. This review does not need to become an overwhelming task. Every learner's file does not need to be updated every day, or even every class. Establishing an appropriate time frame for data reports would help establish a workflow and an expectation for communication. The school librarian may want to hold a collaboration meeting to determine the most effective means and desired frequency to collect and share data. Making assessment part of the routine of the school librarian strengthens the impact of shared learner assessment. It helps communicate to others in the school community the instructional role of the school librarian.

Learner Assessment to Document Impact on Student Achievement

Shared data systems and updated assessment records are each important components of assessment documentation. School librarians who implement these assessment practices can provide data when developing rich, evidence-based discussions about learner progress during school library instruction. Used in this way, learner assessments can be specifically designed to highlight how the school librarian uses assessment to document learner achievement when examining the librarian's own practice.

School librarians can then use learner assessments as part of their data and documentation for evaluation. The learner assessment data collected can highlight areas of focus for program improvement and facilitate conversations with administrators about the impact of school library lessons on learner progress. Learner assessments can also serve as benchmarks toward achievement of a developed school librarian SMART goal that maps learner progress toward mastery. Using assessment data to communicate school library impact allows the school librarian to demonstrate growth of learners across longer spans of time and documents the instructional role of the school librarian in a measurable way.

Assessment Data to Guide Purposeful Instruction

Learner assessment is a key instructional consideration for school librarians seeking to improve and inform learner engagement and progress. Using a variety of ways to monitor and evaluate learner growth through effective and authentic assessment tasks allows school librarians the opportunity to ensure that all learners meet their personal learning targets. Implementation strategies document learner progress and the impact of the school library on integrated learning goals supported across the curriculum.

Learner achievement can be a powerful means to inform the role of library instruction. The use of learner assessment strategies guides library instruction in a purposeful way. Thoughtful selection of learner assessments can provide systematic and effective data to inform and document the impact on learner growth.

Through use of learner assessment, the school librarian is able to operationalize the Competencies in the *AASL Standards Framework for Learners* to measure library learning objectives. This engagement provides the opportunity to alter perceptions on student success and reframe learning in the school library, allowing the school librarian to truly transform teaching and learning.

WORKS CITED

AASL American Association of School Librarians. 2018a. *AASL Standards Framework for Learners*. standards.aasl.org/wp-content/uploads/2017/11/AASL-Standards -Framework-for-Learners-pamphlet.pdf.

AASL American Association of School Librarians. 2018b. *National School Library Standards for Learners, School Librarians, and School Libraries*. Chicago: ALA Editions.

AASL American Association of School Librarians. 2020. "The Instructional Role of the School Librarian Position Statement." ala.org/aasl/sites/ala.org.aasl/files/content/ advocacy/statements/docs/AASL_Position_Statement_Instructional_Role.pdf.

CCSS Common Core State Standards Initiative. 2010a. *Common Core State Standards for English Language Arts and Literacy in History/Social Studies, Science, and Technical Subjects*. learning.ccsso.org/wp-content/uploads/2022/11/ELA_Standards1.pdf.

CCSS Common Core State Standards Initiative. 2010b. *Common Core State Standards for Mathematics*. learning.ccsso.org/wp-content/uploads/2022/11/Math_Standards1 .pdf.

Dweck, Carol S. 2006. *Mindset: The New Psychology of Success*. New York: Random House.

ISTE International Society for Technology in Education. 2016. *ISTE Standards: Students*. iste.org/standards/iste-standards-for-students.

Meyer, I. H., S. Schwartz, and D. M. Frost. 2008. "Social Patterning of Stress and Coping: Does Disadvantaged Social Statuses Confer More Stress and Fewer Coping Resources?" *Social Science and Medicine* 67:368–79.

Mueller, J. 2009. *Assessing Critical Skills*. Linworth Books.

National Research Council. 2013. *Next Generation Science Standards: For States, By States*. Washington, DC: National Academies Press. nextgenscience.org.

NCSS National Council for the Social Studies. 2013. *College, Career, and Civic Life (C3) Framework for Social Studies State Standards: Guidance for Enhancing the Rigor of K–12 Civics, Economics, Geography, and History*. socialstudies.org/sites/default/ files/2017/Jun/c3-framework-for-social-studies-rev0617.pdf.

INDEX

An italicized page number indicates an illustration.